WITHDRAWN

Ripley's Believe It or Not!

Developed and produced by Ripley Publishing Ltd

This edition published and distributed by:
Mason Crest Publishers Inc.
370 Reed Road, Broomall, Pennsylvania 19008
(866) MCP-BOOK (toll free)
www.masoncrest.com

Ripley's Believe It or Not!
Wonders of Science
ISBN 978-1-4222-1545-6
Library of Congress Cataloging-in-Publication data is available

Ripley's Believe It or Not!—Complete 16 Title Series
ISBN 978-1-4222-1529-6

PUBLISHER'S NOTE
While every effort has been made to verify the accuracy of the entries in this book,
the Publishers cannot be held responsible for any errors contained in the work.
They would be glad to receive any information from readers.

WARNING
Some of the stunts and activities in this book are undertaken by experts and should not
be attempted by anyone without adequate training and supervision.

Printed in the United States of America

Believe It or Not!®

WONDERS OF SCIENCE

PUBLISHING

a Jim Pattison Company

Wonders of Science

is a collection of mind-blowing facts about people who have pushed the boundaries of science to its limits and beyond. Read about a featherless chicken, an underwater post office, and the hotel made entirely from ice—all in this unbelieveable book.

Cycling parachutists take to the skies...

The Million-Pound Pound

When Simon Whitaker from Oxfordshire, England, placed a £1 coin (about $1.50) for sale on the eBay auction website, he never expected to face a whopping potential £1 million profit!

What began as a joke escalated fast after Whitaker's friend suggested he contact British national newspaper *The Sun* to record the event. Soon afterwards, offers started to flood onto the auction site for £20, £90, £120, £200—up to a phenomenal £19,500! However, just when things couldn't get any more ridiculous, on the eighth day of bidding an offer came in for over £1 million ($1.5 million)! Realizing the potential fees he stood to pay eBay in the unlikely event the sale actually went through, Whitaker cancelled the auction.

Prior to the story of Simon Whitaker's auction appearing in the news, the pound coin had only received sensible offers in the region of 10–15 pence (14–20 cents).

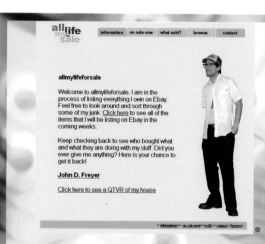

Assessing Self-Worth

To test the value of his life, student John D. Freyer of Iowa undertook a project in 2001 to sell off all his possessions, and even his friends! His website—allmylifeforsale.com—listed all the items he had for sale, from clothes and toilet paper to a tape from his answering machine that included a message from his mother. Other items listed were a 1970s-style telephone, a photocopier, and even his childhood teeth! The most popular of the items for sale, however, were experiences such as a hot-tub session or a dinner date with one of his friends. The aim of the project was to determine how much the life of a student is worth.

John Freyer's website was linked to eBay, so that potential bidders could log onto the auction site and start bidding for any of the items listed on his website. On his site, each item was cataloged with a brief description of how he came to acquire it and any stories linked with it.

DEAD COURIERS

American cartoon artist Paul Kinsella has set up a website where the living can send telegrams to the dead. It costs around $5 per word to post a message, which is then given to a terminally-ill person who memorizes it to take into the afterlife. All recipients must have been dead for at least 30 days.

Txt Wdng :>) A Norwegian couple who met via text messaging got married in an Oslo phone booth in 2003. Long-distance lovers Grete Myrslett and Frode Stroemsoe conducted their romance by phone and picked out their wedding rings before ever meeting in person. The 100 wedding invitations were all sent by text message.

Go to Your Room! In 2002, Chris Phillips from Hampshire, England, worked from his bedroom to set up his own Internet business while still in school. A year later, at 18 years old, he sold 90 percent of the company, which now employs over 100 staff and has seven offices based in the U.S.A. and Canada, for a staggering $2.8 million (£2 million)!

No Joke Scientists in Australia have developed software that allows people to log on to computers by laughing.

"*analyzing dogs' voices*"

Skysurfers Tim Porter and Chris Gauge took the concept of "surfing the net" to a new level when they attached a laptop to one of their boards and attempted to send an Internet message while in freefall.

Rent-a-Cow Swiss dairy farmer Paul Wyler has posted photos of his cows on the Internet with the idea of renting the animals out to cheese-lovers.

Japanese toymaker Takara developed a gadget to enable owners to understand their dogs. "Bowlingual" analyzes a dog's bark and various other noises using a wireless microphone on the dog's collar.

Zoologist Dr. Susan Savage-Rumbaugh has devised a method of communication for the ape world. Her research has proved that it is possible to teach chimpanzees how to communicate by using symbols as part of sign language.

Pot Luck A coffee pot bought ten years ago for $35 (£25) by computer students at Cambridge University, England, became such cult viewing on the Internet that it recently sold for $4,750 (£3,350)! Tired of trekking through their seven-story building only to find the coffee pot empty, the students had set up one of the first webcams so that they could watch it without leaving their desks. The pot became a huge hit as hundreds of thousands of net surfers logged onto the image from all over the world.

Ringing Revenge In 2003, U.S. columnist Dave Barry got his revenge on telesales firms by publishing the phone number of the American Telesales Association in *The Miami Herald* and urging readers to call them. Thousands took his advice, forcing ATA to stop answering the phone!

Safe Siesta There are more telephones in New York City alone than there are in the whole of Spain!

Inflated Bill A man from Yorkshire, England, received a gas bill for a staggering $3.2 million (£2.3 million) in 2003 after a computer mix-up. When the gas company was told of the man's complaint, they checked the error and revised the bill to the princely sum of $85 (£59).

SEX CHANGE
Internet users in China can buy voice-altering machines that make a man sound like a woman and vice-versa. The devices, which hook up to a telephone, cost $12 each and have been selling well, mainly to people trying to find out whether their partner is up for an affair.

Take my Dad Nina Gronland of Trondheim, Norway, was so irritated by her father living with her that she decided to put him up for auction on an Internet site! The ad for 52-year-old cab driver Odd Kristiansen read: "Giving away my dad to a nice woman in Trondheim. Dad is tall, dark, and slim and in his best age. I am tired of him living with me. Furniture comes with him. Serious!"

Saved in Seconds A church in Hokksund, Norway, offers salvation in 12 seconds to anyone who reads a prayer on its website.

BUY A USED TOWN
The Northern California town of Bridgeville became the first town to be sold online when it was bought by a mystery bidder on the Internet auction site eBay for nearly $1.8 million in December 2002. With 82 acres (33 ha), Bridgeville comes complete with a post office, a cemetery, and more than a dozen cabins and houses. It was put up for sale when the previous owners couldn't afford the $200,000 needed to renovate the town. Bidding started at $5,000 and almost 250 bids were made, comfortably exceeding the asking price of $775,000.

"Northern California town sold online for $1.8 million"

Champion Surfers The U.S.A. holds the record for surfing the Internet, coming in at just over 24 percent of the world's total usage.

Hot Mail The amount of junk mail that Americans receive in one day could produce sufficient energy to heat 250,000 homes.

Tired of being asked when he was going to settle down and marry, David Weinlick plucked a date out of thin air—June 13, 1998. At 28 years old, with the deadline looming and no bride in sight, he decided to advertise for her on the Internet! His friends and family picked the bride from an adventurous list of candidates following a session of interviews. Elizabeth Runze was the lucky one who got to walk down the aisle in the Minneapolis shopping mall, just hours after meeting David for the first time ever!

Bliss Online From the start of 2004, couples in Russia have been able to wed via the Internet.

Bride's Net Profit A Florida woman surfing the Internet was stunned to find that her boyfriend had posted a marriage proposal to her on it. Natalie Thilem of Fort Lauderdale was looking for jewelry on the eBay website when she found attached to a heart-shaped diamond engagement ring a proposal from Shane Bushman. She said yes!

An Islamic court ruling decreed that it is acceptable for a man to divorce his wife by sending her a text message, reading "I divorce you" three times.

Doctor Flies to the Rescue

When Scottish surgeon Angus Wallace stepped on board his flight from Hong Kong to London in 1995, he was unaware that he was just hours away from having to perform major surgery on a fellow passenger—using only a coat hanger and various other rudimentary tools.

Professor Angus Wallace carried out the operation using a catheter, brandy bottle, tools from a medical kit, and a wire coat hanger, all found on board the airplane.

AGE OLD CURES

- Whooping cough—Passing a child three times under the belly of a donkey
- Meningitis—Split a pigeon in half and lay the two parts, cut side down, on top of the patient's head
- Toothache—Romans used to strap toads to their jaws
- Diarrhea—An early form of tomato ketchup was a popular cure in the late 19th century
- Respiratory problems—Carrying a child through a flock of sheep
- Rheumatism—A familiar medieval cure was to carry a dead shrew in your pocket

A healthy passenger doesn't feel any effect from reduced air pressure, but Paula Dixon had previously suffered a collapsed lung as a result of a motorbike crash, and so was susceptible to respiratory problems. Wallace had to relieve a tension pneumothorax—air trapped as a result of a malfunction inside the lung—using only the tools available to him on board the plane. The operation was a complete success and Wallace later received a professional award for the act.

Part-time Moms In 1936, at the age of 17, Louise Madeline Pittman of Atlanta, Georgia, decided to divide her time between two sets of parents because a hospital mix-up when she was born made it impossible to determine her real mother.

Fare Hearing In 1995, doctors in Sweden restored a deaf man's hearing by removing a bus ticket that had been lodged in his ear for 47 years!

Dangerous Weapon Every year around 8,800 people are injured using toothpicks.

Grrr! Actress Sarah Bernhardt once consulted a doctor about having the tail of a tiger grafted to the base of her spine.

Dimbeswar Basumatary from India has amazed doctors by being able to stare at the Sun for hours on end without so much as blinking! Of course this should never ever be attempted by anyone!

Deadening the Pain An Argentinean man was refused treatment for toothache in 2002 because his medical records showed that he had died in 1980! Rafael Lanizante thought it was a joke until he saw his own death certificate. While the mix-up was investigated, there was at least some good news from Mr. Lanizante—with all the confusion, his toothache had disappeared!

Sick Bets In 1980, a Las Vegas hospital suspended workers for placing bets on when patients would die.

GIVING HIS ALL

General Francis T. Nicholls lost his left arm at the Battle of Winchester, in 1862, and his left foot at Chancellorsville in 1863, yet continued to serve as a Confederate officer until the end of the U.S. Civil War. In 1876, he was elected Governor of Louisiana, having offered voters "what is left of General Nicholls."

Deep Bite When Kevin Morrison of Rockford, Illinois, was bitten by a 3-ft (1-m) nurse shark in 1998, doctors had to surgically remove the shark from his chest.

Slow Bullet Bruce Levon of Gross Pointe, Michigan, was accidentally shot in the head in 1983—but didn't know it until doctors spotted the slug in an X-ray eight years later!

Have You Had Your Head Examined?

Believe it or not, this bizarre machine was used to determine a person's health and happiness! The wire cage fitted over the head and the machine "read" bumps on the sitter's head. A print-out displayed the development of each of the 32 faculties that believers felt determined the well-being of a person. This pseudo-science, known as phrenology, was used to determine the best presidential candidate in the 1848 election. Zachary Taylor won but died soon after.

Made in about 1908, this machine purported to be able to determine the sitter's well-being.

A side-show tent erected in the early part of the 20th century housed phrenologists who made a living by carrying out readings.

BREASTFED BY DAD

In 2002, it was reported that a Sri Lankan man, whose wife died while giving birth to their second child, was able to breastfeed his elder daughter. Mr. B. Wijeratne from Walapanee, near Colombo, discovered his talent after his 18-month-old daughter Nisansala refused to take formula milk. He said: "She was used to her mother's milk and rejected the powdered milk so I tried feeding through a bottle. Unable to see her cry, I offered my breast. That's when I discovered that I could breastfeed her." Doctors say that men with a hyperactive prolactine hormone are able to produce breast milk.

This pacemaker, worn by Scott McIver, is the size of a U.K. 50 pence piece. The first ever pacemaker was too large to fit in the human body!

Talked to Death Edward Dilly (1732–79) of London, England, never stopped talking—even in his sleep. Physicians certified this as his actual cause of death.

It took 600 hours to create this skeleton inside a bottle! The bones were carved from hard maple wood and then dropped through the narrow neck and assembled inside the bottle.

Out-of-Date A Roman metal pot unearthed at an archeological dig in London in 2003 was found to contain 2,000-year-old ointment.

Left Right, Left Right A French woman was born in 1869 with two pelvises and four legs. She married and gave birth to two normal children.

Sleepless in Romania In December 2003, doctors in Budeasa, Romania, were mystified by a woman who claimed not to have slept for eight years. Maria Stelica, 58, developed insomnia when her mother died in 1995 and had stayed awake ever since.

Self Scan Dale Eller, 22, walked into a police station in Columbus, Ohio, in 1990 and requested an X-ray to locate his brain. He showed baffled officers a hole in his skull, which he said he had made with a power drill, and through which he had inserted a 3-in (8-cm) piece of wire in a failed attempt to find his brain. Surgeons later removed part of a wire coat hanger from his head.

Persistent Patient Between 1929 and 1979, British hypochondriac William McIlroy underwent 400 operations and stayed at over 100 different hospitals, using 22 aliases.

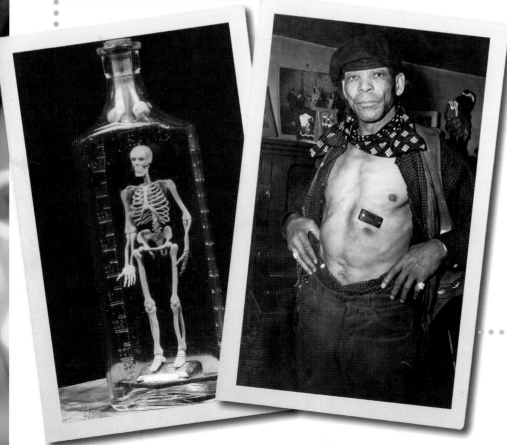

Sioux "Chief" Couzzingo, from Oxford, Ohio, fastened his broken rib to his breastbone using a screwdriver—without anesthetic!

Hiro Takeuchi works for the Hello Tomorrow and New Body Institute in Japan, where he creates artificial human body parts from silicon and vinyl chloride. These parts, which include ears, breasts, legs, and arms, are bought for 30,000 yen ($300) or more, by people who have lost body parts through disease or accident.

Channel Flipper Bryan Allison, 24, was hospitalized in Buffalo, New York, in 2001 after falling 20 ft (6 m) while throwing a television set from the second-floor balcony of his home. He was watching a videotape replay of a 1989 National Hockey League playoff game and became incensed once again that his team had lost. Angrily, he picked up the TV set and hurled it off the balcony—but forgot to let go!

Hart of the Problem Dianne Neale, a 49-year-old American, suffered epileptic seizures in 1991 whenever she heard the voice of *Entertainment Tonight* host Mary Hart. The TV presenter even apologized on air for the distress she caused her!

CHOCOLATES TO LIVE FOR German confectioner Adolf Andersen believes he has created the world's first anti-ageing chocolates. He claims the ingredients in Felice pralines—dark chocolate, mango, and soya milk—not only make you happy, but immediately make you feel 15 years younger.

John Evans suffered severe injuries after he was struck by a train. He woke up to find his left hand had been attached to his right arm!

TV Seizure At 6.50 p.m. on December 16, 1997, 685 people in Japan, mostly children, simultaneously suffered epileptic seizures. After an investigation, it transpired that they had all been watching the television cartoon *Pocket Monsters*, and that the seizures had been caused by the program's flashing red and blue lights.

Feeling the Heat The highest manufactured temperature was created by scientists at Princeton University in 1978. They managed to generate a temperature of 70 million degrees Celsius!

Spoken Word Scientists have created a machine that scans the words of a book, no matter what typeface, and feeds the information into a computer, which translates it into spoken English for the visually impaired.

Gene Jugglers

The new breed of featherless chicken, developed in Israel, is designed not to suffer from the heat as much as feathered birds do.

While American pet owners clamor for designer dogs such as the Labradoodle (a cross between a Labrador and a poodle), scientists across the world are experimenting with nature to create new cross-breeds.

Israeli scientists recently came up with a bright pink featherless chicken, its ugliness offset by the fact that it doesn't need plucking. And in August 2003, a Japanese safari park unveiled the world's only living zenkey—an animal that looks like a donkey in pyjamas, as well it might since it is a cross between a donkey and a zebra.

Developed in Dubai, the "cama"—half camel, half llama—is the first of its kind!

SCIENCE FACTS

- Peanuts are an ingredients used to make explosives

- Our atmosphere is showered every 24 hours by 750,000,000,000,000,000 meteors

- Fragments of breaking glass can move at up to 3,000 mph (4,800 km/h)

- All the gold that has ever been mined in the world to date would only make a block the size of a tennis court and as high as a 400 oz (11,340 g) gold bar

- A hit golf ball spins about 8,000 revolutions a minute

The "zenkey," developed in Japan, has a donkey mother and a zebra father.

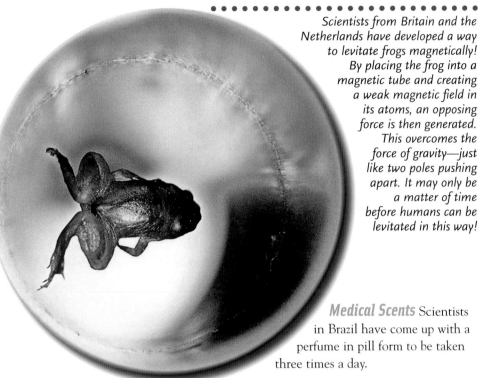

Scientists from Britain and the Netherlands have developed a way to levitate frogs magnetically! By placing the frog into a magnetic tube and creating a weak magnetic field in its atoms, an opposing force is then generated. This overcomes the force of gravity—just like two poles pushing apart. It may only be a matter of time before humans can be levitated in this way!

Medical Scents Scientists in Brazil have come up with a perfume in pill form to be taken three times a day.

Shaky Robot In 1992, scientists in San Francisco invented a robot that could mix 150 different drinks and add up the bar tab!

Naval Campaign Karl Kruszelnicki, a scientist at the University of Sydney, Australia, has written a study of belly-button fluff after examining samples from 5,000 people.

A Drop in the Ocean Scientists calculate there are roughly the same number of molecules in a spoonful of water as there are spoonfuls of water in the Atlantic Ocean.

SCHOOL OF FISH
Scientists at Plymouth University, England, claim that fish can tell the time. They trained fish that were kept in a tank to feed themselves by pressing a lever to release the food. Although food was only available for one hour, the fish quickly figured out when it would arrive. Experts had recently proved that fish had at least a three-month memory.

Dodging Raindrops Scientists Trevor Wallis and Thomas Peterson of the National Climatic Data Center in Asheville, North Carolina, have discovered that a person walking in the rain gets 40 percent wetter than a person who runs in it.

Gone But Not Forgotten
The Tasmanian tiger was declared extinct in 1936, but a pup preserved in ethanol for 130 years may hold the key to reviving the species. Australian scientists have successfully replicated DNA from the specimen and plan to bring the species back from extinction!

The Tasmanian tiger has not been seen for over 70 years, but scientists now hope to recreate the animal within the next ten years.

The preserved Tasmanian tiger pup is the key to the revival of the species.

ROBO DANCER

Japanese scientists have developed a dancing robot that is capable of following a human dancer's lead. The Mobile Smart Dance Robot predicts the dancer's next move through hand pressure applied to its back. Equipped with a computer, sensor, batteries, and four wheels, it can move in any direction and has enough memory for the necessary steps to dance a waltz.

Pages with Half-Life The notebooks in which Marie and Pierre Curie recorded details of their experiments on radium nearly 100 years ago are still dangerously radioactive.

Two climbers in the Oetztaler Alps discovered a glacier-mummy—a freeze-dried man. "Otzi," as he was called, had been preserved in ice for about 5,000 years at an altitude of about 10,000 ft (3,000 m). Scientists in Italy defrosted him in the hope of learning more about his lifestyle.

Non-Stick In its liquid form, mercury can be poured out of a jug and yet leave the inside of the jug completely dry.

Sniffer Bees Researchers at the University of Montana have been training honeybees to sniff out landmines. Apparently bees not only have a better sense of smell than dogs, but they also learn faster.

Cold Logic Albert Einstein not only developed the Theory of Relativity—he also designed refrigerators!

Bite-Sized To cater for Japan's rising population of single people, scientists have created a range of dwarf vegetables, including mini cauliflowers and half-size radishes.

Bacteria Revival Scientists in Chicago have revived 2,800-year-old frozen bacteria and algae, that were found lying dormant in an Antarctic lake.

German scientist Ursula Plate of the Medical University of Lübeck has developed a cure for those with a fear of flying! The 3-D glasses simulate a turbulent, but safe, flight from Hamburg to Munich.

Carp Get the Beat Scientists at the Rowland Institute for Science in Massachusetts have taught Koi carp to detect the difference between classical music and the blues!

Laid Back Turkeys In the run-up to Christmas, turkey farmers in Britain play "relaxation" CDs to their birds. Farmers suggest that playing music to their turkeys has a calming effect on them and, as a consequence, keeps their meat tender.

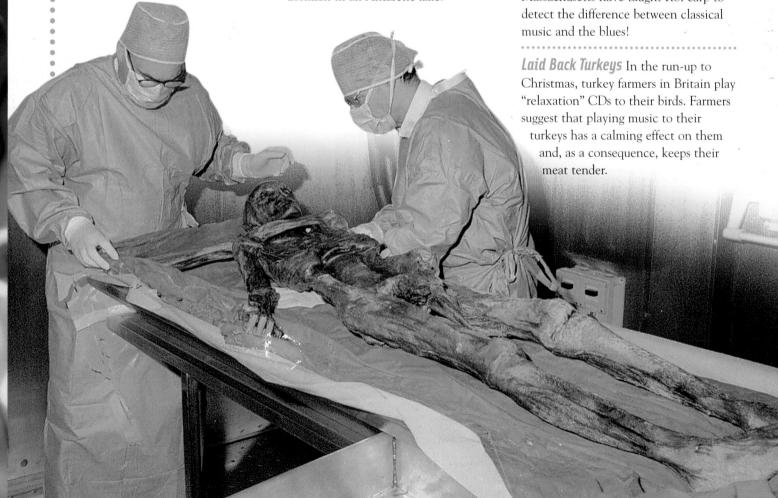

BID FOR FREEDOM

Gaak, a "living robot" programmed to think for itself, made a daring escape from its compound in Rotherham, England, in 2002. It broke out of its paddock, traveled down an access slope, through the front door of the Magna Science Centre, and was eventually discovered at the main entrance to the car park after nearly being run over by a visitor! Professor Noel Sharkey said: "There's no need to worry, as although they can escape they are perfectly harmless and won't be taking over just yet."

Terror of the Roosts Two Scottish inventors have devised a robotic bird of prey designed to scare off pigeons by swooping on their territory. The flying fiberglass peregrine falcon can move its head and call like a real bird. Creator, Bob McIntyre, says, "The bird is very high tech. It can even give you a call on your cell phone to let you know when its battery is running down."

Flylight U.S. government scientists have developed a tiny robotic fly with solar-powered wings that weighs only 0.004 oz (0.1 g)—less than a small size paper clip!

Tattoo on Trust Austrian electrician Niki Passath has created Freddy, the world's first tattooing robot. But you can't choose your design—Freddy's computerized brain, which is programmed with artistic outlines, takes care of that.

Barb's Pills Dr. Adolph Von Baeyer (1835–1917), a chemist in Berlin, Germany, who discovered barbituric acid (which gave us barbiturates) named his find not after an ingredient but in honor of a sweetheart named Barbara!

Numbers Game Benjamin Franklin, the statesman, scientist, and inventor, was born on January 17, 1706, was one of 17 children, started his career in Philadelphia at 17, and died on April 17, 1790.

The almost perfectly preserved skeleton of this meat-eating baby scipionix dinosaur was found intact! Remnants of the liver, large intestine, windpipe, and muscles can even be seen! Scientists understand that it lived approximately 110 million years ago.

No Tip Necessary A hotel in Atlantic City, New Jersey, unveiled Rich, a 5 ft (1.5 m) tall robot whose duties included mingling with guests and delivering room service meals. The management refused to let him gamble in the casino for fears that he could be equipped to cheat with hidden cameras.

The Ignoble Prize You've heard of the Nobel Prize—well this is the Ignoble Prize! Winners must achieve two things: they have to make people laugh, and they have to make them think. Entrants in 2003 for the prizes for physics and medicine categories have submitted reports on "An Analysis of the Forces Required to Drag Sheep over Various Surfaces" and "Navigation-Related Structural change in the Hippocampi of Taxi Drivers."

Faith in the Air

Churchgoers who for years have endured hard, wooden pews may have had their prayers answered by an inflatable church that was developed near London, England.

Apart from the inflatable pews, the 46-ft (14-m) high building contains a blow-up organ, altar, pulpit, candles—even inflatable stained-glass windows! As many as 60 worshipers can fit into the invention.

Visitors try the seats of the inflatable church on display at the National Christian Resources Exhibition in 2003!

It takes less than one hour to inflate the plastic bouncy-church!

Close the Cover Dutch designer Hans Rademaker has created a bookcase that can be converted into a coffin after the owner's death.

Let's Call it a Vodka In 1997, researchers at the University of Idaho developed a cold-climate potato that produces its own antifreeze.

Who Needs a Wife? A German firm has built the first talking washing machine. Speaking in a friendly female voice, "Hermine" gives advice on how to load the machine and get the best results from the wash. She can also understand complex spoken commands.

Backyard Snow A U.S. company sells a machine that will make real snow in your yard overnight!

PROBLEM LICKED
Rick Hartman, a toymaker from Issaquah, Washington, has invented a motorized ice cream holder in order to eliminate tongue stress caused from licking ice cream. "Ice-cream technology has been stagnant for the last 200 years," says Hartman. A motor inside an acrylic cone is connected to an activator button, which, when pressed, makes the cone whirl without the tongue moving.

The invention of the snowshoe was displayed by Charlie Miller, a famous guide from Boston, who walked 223 mi (360 km) on them!

Eat it All Researchers at Campinas State University in Sao Paulo, Brazil, have created an edible plastic wrap, made from amaranto flour.

Fear Spray Mary Elizabeth Feldman of Charleston, South Carolina has invented Ghost Away, a chamomile-based spray to use against ghosts and monsters!

Eau de Anything Christopher Brosius of New York City creates fragrances for people who want to smell like lobsters, dandelions, sugar cookies, or even dirt!

Ear Ring Reginald M. Grooms of Conway, South Carolina, invented an alarm clock that is worn inside the ear.

TOP FIVE
AGE-OLD INVENTIONS

Some inventions that are used on a daily basis have been around for an amazingly long time.

1 Comb—*c. 8000* BC

2 Plastic surgery—third century BC

3 Umbrella—second century BC

4 Sleeping pill—first century BC

5 Cook book—AD 62

Wake-up Shoes Scientists at Boston University, Massachusetts, have developed vibrating insoles to be worn inside shoes. The random vibrations amplify balance-related signals between the feet and the brain, which become dulled with age. It is hoped that the new shoes will prevent elderly people from losing their balance and suffering falls.

This 14.8-ft (4.5-m) long vehicle is shaped like a submarine, but the periscope is made from a video camera and the turret from a washing machine! Invented by Jo L'Tessier, the vehicle is powered by electricity and can reach speeds of up to 12 mph (20 km/h)!

The annual International Birdman Festival in Bognor Regis, England, attracts the most inventive minds, including Sir Richard Branson. Entrants create personal flying machines and test them to the limit by jumping off the end of the pier.

New Ideas Not Welcome In 1875, the director of the U.S. Patent Office suggested that the department be closed down because, in his opinion, there was nothing left to invent. How wrong he was!

No Quack-Ups Argentinean inventors have come up with a strap-on rubber duck, which they claim will combat tiredness in drivers. The Duckmaster fastens around the neck and starts quacking if the user's head slumps forward.

Mood Mouse A company in California has developed a computer mouse that can sense the emotions of the person using it. The Emotion Mouse can measure pulse, temperature, and skin resistance to identify states of sadness, happiness, or anger.

Sudden Inflation Japanese inventor Katsu Katugoru, whose greatest fear is drowning, has created inflatable underwear! Inconveniently, the garment accidentally inflated to 30 times its original size in a crowded subway.

For Him! To evoke memories of the celebrated Oktoberfest, Munich's annual homage to beer, German pub landlord Peter Inselkammer has created a new perfume that smells of rancid beer and cigarette butts! It costs around $160 a bottle.

Roll On When Joseph Gayetty invented toilet paper in 1857, he had his name printed on each sheet.

Fear Banished Light bulb inventor Thomas Edison was afraid of the dark.

Hot Table Richard E. Mahan of Houston, Texas, invented an electrified tablecloth to stop insects landing near the food!

These automatic eyeglass cleaners were presented by a hopeful Indian student for the Young Inventor Award in Bangalore.

Make a Note! Laszlo Biro, inventor of the ballpoint pen, lost a fortune by forgetting to patent it in the U.S.A.

PIZZA BUBBLES
Ducio Cresci, a cosmetics manufacturer from Florence, Italy, has devised a new range of bathroom products that smell like pizza. Using tomato extract plus essential oils of basil and oregano, he has created a luxury bubble bath, soap, and body lotion—all with the great aroma of pizza. He says: "The bubble bath smells especially strong when you are bathing in it, but once out of the water it leaves an irresistible trace of scent on your skin." Cresci, a former TV presenter, has not stopped there. His Experimenta range also includes cappuccino soap, baked Tuscan bread body lotion, and oils smelling of chocolate, cake, and chewing gum.

Plenty of Pin Money In 1849, the safety pin was created by New York mechanic Walter Hunt—by accident. He was idly twisting a wire while trying to think of something that would enable him to pay off his $15 debt.

For Dunkers Dominic Skinner from England invented a coffee cup with a built-in cookie shelf to store three cookies—without getting them soggy.

First Shoe-Trees Rubber shoes were first made in Brazil around 1820 by tapping a rubber tree and letting the liquid latex drop on the bare feet of local workers! After the rubber dried, the shoes were removed and exported to the U.S. for sale.

"Pyon-pyon" or hopping shoes are a recent creation from Japanese Dr. Joshino Nakamatsu, who already has an astonishing 2,300 patents to his name. Made of plastic with a spring to disperse the weight of the wearer, they put a bounce back into your step.

Flying Papers In 1972 Robert Lamar of Houston, Texas, patented a design for a truck that would automatically throw newspapers onto subscribers' lawns.

Ideas in Motion Acting on the theory that physical stimulation of the buttocks helps relieve constipation, in 1966 U.S. inventor Thomas J. Bayard invented a vibrating toilet seat.

Needle Point In 1914, Natalie Stolp of Philadelphia devised an implement designed to discourage men from rubbing a leg against a lady's thigh on a crowded train or carriage. A spring attached to the lady's underskirt responded to pressure by releasing a short, sharp point into the offender's flesh.

The donut was invented by a sea captain to fit the handle of a steering wheel. During a storm in 1850 Captain Hanson Gregory, skipper of the good ship Donat, squeezed a "solid sinker" weight down over a wheel handle in order to keep both hands free to steer the ship, and so the donut was born!

Cleaning the toilet seat has never been easier than with Swiss inventor Juerg Lumpert's "disinfection element." The clean-crazy creation uses an ultraviolet wavelength of light, which hovers above the seat, negating the need for disinfectant.

"cleaning the toilet using hovering lightwaves"

Tin Boat Hovercraft inventor, Christopher Cockerell, constructed his prototype model from an empty can of cat food, a coffee can, and a vacuum cleaner.

For Stepping Out An Australian inventor has developed pantyhose that have three legs—in case one of the other two gets a run.

A Head of Beer Randy Flann of Milwaukee, Wisconsin, has invented headgear that comes in the shape of a football, a baseball, or a basketball, and also a keg that contains beer!

No Wet Dogs Celes Antoine of Forestville, Maryland, invented a self-supported umbrella for dogs!

Pecking Order In 1902, Andrew Jackson Jr. of Tennessee patented an eye protector shaped like a pair of miniature glasses for chickens to prevent them being hen-pecked.

Hats Off! In 1920, Alan Dawson of Jacksonville, Florida, invented a hat with a built-in comb.

Close the Cover In 1986 American Ralph R. Pire of Lindenhurst, New York, devised a mechanical arm apparatus attached to the shoulder that allowed the wearer to pat himself on the back whenever he felt in need of a psychological lift.

This novel, naval invention simulates the rolling and pitching of a ship in a storm and was used to test levels of sea sickness among sailors.

EAR-WAX MIRROR
Justin Letlow from Bend, Oregon has invented an ear mirror to help people clean their ears and avoid "earwax embarrassment." It features two small, adjustable mirrors connected by a flexible plastic handle. Users hold one mirror close to their ear and the other in front of their eyes. Explaining the need for his invention, Mr. Letlow says, "I can't think how many times I've been watching a game on TV, and they zoom in on the coach, and there's this big old piece of earwax."

It's possible to travel at 12 mph (20 km/h) with the Segway™ Human Transporter, invented by Dean Kamen. It is a two-wheel vehicle with powerful motors, tilt sensors, and gyroscopes to detect your center of gravity.

Floating Furniture In 1989 William A. Calderwood, of Arizona, devised a range of helium-filled furniture, tethered to the floor that, when not in use, could float up to the ceiling!

The New Black A group of scientists have developed a new paint color—superblack. It's blacker in hue than all other blacks and absorbs 99.7 percent of light, so almost no light is reflected from its surface.

Kissing Shield For those who enjoy kissing but dread the thought of catching a disease, Deloris Gray Wood of Missouri has invented the kissing shield. A thin, latex membrane stretched over an attractive heart-shaped frame, the shield is worn over the mouth and is described by its inventor as being ideal for vote-hungry politicians who have to kiss a lot of babies.

French physician Dr. Theophile de Laennec (1781–1826) invented the stethoscope in 1814 to spare the feelings of a modest female patient while listening to her heartbeat. He rolled a sheet of paper into a cone.

"Qrio," a humanoid robot, shows off its amazingly human flexibility and ability to dance! It weighs just 15 lbs (7 kg), is 23 in (58 cm) tall and was presented at the Robodex exhibition in 2003!

Santa Detector American inventor Thomas Cane has come up with a device to ensure that children no longer miss the arrival of Santa Claus. A wired stocking is hung over the fireplace and as soon as Santa emerges from the chimney, lights on the stocking start flashing to wake the children of the house.

Animal Lover In 1999, American inventor Stephen B. Hoy devised an edible greeting card for pets.

Safety First To reduce pedestrian casualties in 1960, David Gutman from Philadelphia invented a special bumper to be fixed to the front of cars. The bumper not only cushioned any impact but also had a huge pair of claws that grabbed the pedestrian around the waist to prevent him falling to the ground.

Special Delivery

In September 2003 Charles McKinley shipped himself from New Jersey to Dallas in an airline cargo crate because he thought it was the cheapest way to fly.

The 25-year-old shipping clerk made the unscheduled trip because he was homesick and a friend told him he could save money by flying as cargo, although in fact he could have flown first class for the same cost if he had realized how much he would have to pay in fines! Before climbing into the crate, McKinley filled out forms saying it contained a computer and clothing. The box was loaded onto a pressurized cargo plane and flew from Newark, New Jersey, to Niagara Falls, New York, then to Fort Wayne, Indiana, before continuing to Dallas. The courier who delivered the crate to McKinley's parents' home first became suspicious when he thought he saw a pair of eyes peering out. He feared it contained a dead body until, in front of his startled parents, McKinley broke out of the box on their doorstep. After the courier alerted the police, District Attorney Bill Hill said of McKinley: "He violated the law of stupidity if nothing else."

Stowaway Charles McKinley went without food or water for the 15-hour journey home to Dallas, Texas. The crate in which he stowed away was just 5 ft 8 in (1.7 m) tall.

WEIRD CARGO

- Eileen Cresswell, a 63-year-old grandmother, was arrested for masterminding an international drug smuggling plot

- A student smuggled a tortoise into England—inside his sock!

- A Swedish tourist tried to smuggle eight baby snakes, including four venemous king cobras, into Australia

- A U.S. man was arrested after trying to smuggle four pigeons into Canada under his shirt

The Solar Challenge attracts hundreds of solar-powered cars from across the world to compete in the 2,300-mi (3,700-km) race.

Foul Cargo In 2003 customs officers at Amsterdam's Schiphol airport in the Netherlands opened a smelly suitcase—and found it full of rotting baboon noses!

Jumbo Fuel Bill A full jumbo jet tank contains enough fuel to drive the average car around the world four times.

Watery Graveyard Over 1,500 shipwrecks lie in the waters surrounding New York Harbor.

TICKET FLURRY

Walter H. Burtin of Washington, D.C., was arrested and charged with committing 34 traffic offences in ten minutes—he passed 15 red lights and nine stop signs, disregarded four official signs, twice drove on the wrong side of the street, drove through a safety zone, failed to slow down at an intersection, drove without a permit, and was caught speeding.

Israeli newlyweds buck the traditional modes of transportation to travel to their wedding reception on a plow!

Short Hop The shortest scheduled flight in the world is British Airways' twice-daily flight between the islands of Westray and Papa Westray off the north coast of Scotland. It takes just two minutes to reach its destination!

Baboon at the Switch At Uitenhage Station, South Africa, a baboon once stood in for a crippled signalman. The intelligent ape infallibly operated six levers as it was directed.

Over the Limit In 1903 England became the first country to impose a speed restriction on the road. Vehicles were limited to 20 mph (32 km/h).

No Frills Flight In May 2003 the world's maiden naked flight carried 87 nude passengers from Miami, Florida to Cancun, Mexico. Arranged by a travel agency specializing in naturism, all the passengers except for the captain and the crew stripped off their clothes when the plane reached its cruising altitude.

A staggering 500,000 stamps have been painstakingly stuck to this VW Beetle, exhibited at an international stamp fair in Germany.

Horse Power Today, a rocket can fly to the Moon quicker than an 1800s stagecoach could travel from one end of England to the other.

Don't Look Up On August 27, 1933, Lieutenant Tito Falconi of the Italian Air Force flew a plane from St. Louis, Missouri, to Joilet, Illinois—a distance of 250 mi (402 km)—in 3hr 6 min 30 sec—flying the entire journey upside down.

Burning Up the Road A 3-mi (5-km) long road in Orchard, Texas, was built of sulphuric slag, and when it rained the hot exhaust pipes of automobiles set it on fire.

A streetcar invented by I. Mathewson of Gilroy, California, in 1876 had its gasoline motor disguised as the head of a horse so that it would not frighten real horses!

Cracking Cheeses During a vital wartime engagement between the fleets of Uruguay and Argentina in 1841, the Uruguayan flagship *Santa Maria* ran out of cannon balls. So the ship's American commander, John Coe, ordered the guns to be loaded instead with hard Dutch cheeses, and the Argentinean navy was routed!

Costly Number Sichuan Airlines of China paid $190,000 for the phone number 8888-8888 in the hope that it would make its customers happy. The number eight is considered lucky because it sounds like the Chinese word for "getting rich."

Olive Squeeze American Airlines saved an estimated $40,000 in 1987 by removing one olive from each salad served with first-class meals.

Light Lunch Charles Lindbergh took only four sandwiches with him for sustenance on his famous transatlantic flight.

"Best Lowrider Car" "Best Hopping" and "Best Car Dancing" are just some of the competitions the Lowrider Experience exhibitors can enter. They can also show off their luxury interiors.

This 115-ft (35-m) long sofa was constructed for European Car Free Day in Italy, in 2001, during which members of the public protested against too many cars on the road. The sofa seated more than 100 people.

Anti-Clamp Crusader

In 2003 a man wearing a Superman-style costume roamed the streets of London, England, illegally freeing wheel-clamped cars—with an angle grinder.

Under the guise of Angle Grinder Man, he illegally released at least 12 cars in the capital. He even set up his own Angle Grinder Man website with a call-out number for clamped motorists. "I'm performing a public service," said the anonymous crusader. "And I like wearing the costume."

Monster Jam A 1980 traffic jam stretched 109 mi (175 km) northwards from Lyon in France.

Drinks Caddy Bill Francis of Lakewood, Colorado, turned a 1964 Cadillac car into a full-sized bar in his recreation room.

Holy Rollers Romanian priests bless cars in the belief that it will make the vehicles safer on the roads. The ceremony involves splashing holy water on the engine and seats of the car.

TRAVEL-LOG

- One in 300 of all road accidents in Canada involves a moose
- There are approximately 800,000 people flying in airplanes around the world at any given moment
- The wingspan of a Boeing 747 is longer than the length of the Wright Brothers' maiden flight
- In Ethiopia there is just one car for every 1,468 people
- Car airbags inflate at 200 mph (322 km/h)

Angle Grinder Man—the auto hero who illegally freed wheel-clamped cars using an angle grinder.

Tandem sport takes on a new meaning when parachutists take to the skies while riding a bicycle!

No Ewe Turn As part of a 1996 safety initiative, authorities in the Dutch town of Culemburg released six sheep into their busy streets to control the speed of rush-hour traffic!

Women's Touch In 1955 Chrysler developed a car called the Dodge La Femme that was to be sold exclusively to women. The car came with a matching purse, umbrella, and raincoat!

Risky Front Seat In 2003 a woman was arrested for dangerous driving after she drove 2 mi (3 km) to a police station in Dubrovnik, Croatia, with her drunken husband on the car hood!

Last Laugh A Romanian man was so upset at failing his driving test that he set his car on fire. He said: "When I came home I thought I saw the car laughing at me. So I put gas on it and lit it up."

Bean Power In Brazil in times of crop surplus, coffee beans were used to power steam locomotives.

Winding Roads If all the roads in the United States were joined together, they would encircle the globe 150 times.

Undertaken A Dutch hearse driver was fired in 2003 for losing a coffin on the way to a funeral.

Going in Style Betty Young was buried at Phillips Memorial Cemetery in Foster, Rhode Island, inside her 1989 Cadillac Coupe de Ville!

Hello Dolly Arlene Lambert of Toronto, Ontario, drives a car that is covered with hundreds of plastic baby dolls.

Ripley's
GIANT RUBBER TIRE
EXHIBIT NO: 15280
MEASURES 12 FT 10 IN (4 M) IN DIAMETER, IS 137 IN (54 IN) WIDE AND WEIGHS 12,000 LBS (5,440 KG)

This is the world's largest tire and costs $30,000 to produce. There is enough rubber in one of these tires to make 5,276 average-sized car tires! It takes three days to make one tire and can support 250,000 lbs (113,400 kg). They are used on front-end loader Caterpillars, which are used in open pit mining.

Head for Heights

To 41-year-old Frenchman Alain Robert, tall buildings are personal challenges. He climbs their outside surfaces to dizzying heights, sticking to glass, brick, concrete, and steel like a human fly—without any safety ropes to keep him from hurtling to his death.

EARLY BOOKING

Dutch architect Hans-Jurgen Rombaut has designed the Moon's first hotel, complete with a low-gravity games area where guests would be able to fly wearing special suits. As there is no wind on the Moon, the building is of a fragile design but it has a thick hull to protect visitors from extreme temperatures and cosmic rays. Guests will stay in teardrop-shaped habitation capsules that hang from two huge pillars to create the impression of constant travel. Rombaut hopes the hotel will be open for business by 2050.

He started climbing at the age of 11 and has scaled more than 60 buildings, using only specially adapted climbing shoes. His claims to fame are conquering the 984-ft (300-m) high Eiffel Tower in Paris, New York's Empire State Building at 1,250 ft (381 m) and the 1,482-ft (452-m) Petronas Twin Towers in Kuala Lumpur, Malaysia.

Alain Robert often dresses as Spiderman for his death-defying climbs.

Nothing Wasted In 2002 Taiwanese researchers unveiled a new house brick made with sludge from sewage works. They said it was a good way of using up waste and insisted that the bricks didn't smell.

God's Glass House Built in 1980 at the behest of TV evangelist Robert Schuller, the $20 million (£11 million) Crystal Cathedral near Los Angeles is made from over 10,000 panes of glass. In fact the only non-glass components were white steel trusses and wooden fittings.

Bombproof The old tower of Grevenmacher in Luxembourg, a part of the town wall erected in 882, was the only structure not demolished by an air raid against the town in 1944. Yet 34 years earlier the tower had been declared unsafe.

Backyard Beacon Denver and Clover Randles of Ohio spent 18 years building a 45-ft (14-m) high lighthouse in their yard, even though they live 400 mi (645 km) from the ocean!

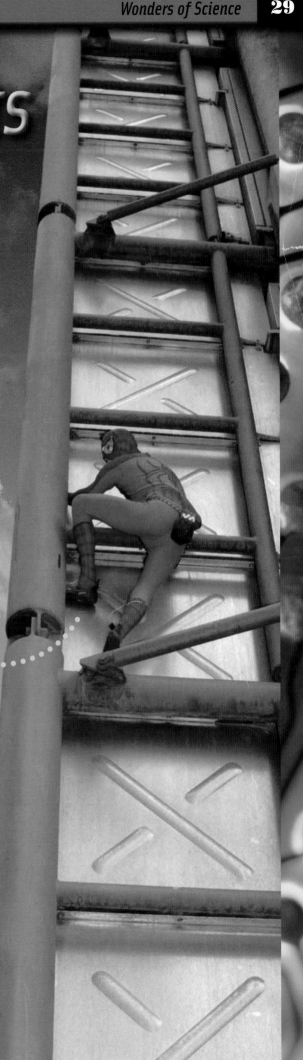

BOTTLED UP

In 1956 Tressa "Grandma" Prisbrey found that her collection of pencils, which eventually numbered 17,000, had outgrown her house trailer in Santa Susana, California. So she began constructing a building to display them, using a material that was cheap and plentiful—discarded bottles. Over the next 25 years she created the Bottle Village, the ultimate recycling venture. As well as collecting bottles, she would visit the local dump to find old tiles and car headlights. When she finished it, the village consisted of 22 buildings, made out of approximately one million bottles set in cement.

Fruit Topping A building in Dunmore Park, Scotland, is topped with a 53-ft (16-m) high stone pineapple.

Waterproof postcards are embossed with waterproof stamps when customers mail them at the aquatic mailbox off the coast of Hideaway Island, Vanuatu. A 9-ft (3-m) dive is needed to reach the postbox first.

Dog Tired A hotel in Vancouver provides a resident dog that guests can book for a stress-relieving stroll.

Full Deck The Pack o' Cards public house in Combe Martin, Devon, England, has 52 windows (the number of playing cards in a pack), four main floors (the number of suits) and 13 doors on the ground floor (the number of cards per suit).

Home to Roost The roof of a house in Santiago, Chile, collapsed in September 2003 under the weight of accumulated pigeon droppings. Ana Maria Bustos said she ended up with a year's worth of pigeon guano on her living-room floor.

Stable Environment Farm animals have been banned from blocks of council flats in the Russian city of Kiev after a survey revealed that residents were keeping over 3,000 pigs, 500 cows and 1,000 goats. The city authorities said that cows were being kept on balconies and even in bedrooms and bathrooms. Unrepentant flat owners pleaded that the animals helped keep the flats warm in winter.

Towering Ambition

In the Watts district of Los Angeles stands a curious monument to the ingenuity and determination of Simon Rodia, an Italian immigrant laborer. Over a period of 33 years, Rodia, working alone, built around his house the Watts Towers. The tallest tower is nearly 100 ft (30 m) high and contains the longest slender column of reinforced concrete in the world. Rodia finally laid down his tools in 1954 at the age of 79, deeded the property to his neighbor for nothing, and disappeared!

Watts Towers comprise nine structures made of steel and mortar.

One of Rodia's towers is embedded with pieces of ceramic tile, pottery shards, sea shells, and broken glass.

Cracking Up Raymond Isidore of Chartres, France, spent a total of 23,000 hours to make his home and all its furnishings out of a million broken dishes.

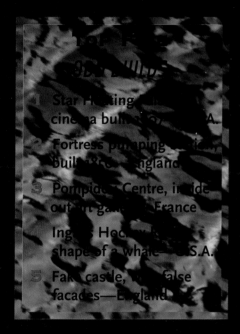

Not to be Forgotten Built at Margate, New Jersey, in 1881 by James V. Lafferty as a real-estate promotion, Lucy the elephant is a 65-ft (20-m) high building of wood and tin. In her time she has served as a tavern and a hotel, and is currently a tourist attraction.

Botched Blast A Romanian wrecking crew failed to demolish an apartment building in the town of Flaminzi in 2001, but their "controlled" explosion left 24 neighboring houses uninhabitable after blowing out every house window within 200 yds (183 m).

High-rise Zoo After neighbors reported hearing roars coming from their Manhattan apartment tower in 2003, police found a 400-lbs (180 kg) male tiger being kept as a pet in a tiny fifth-floor apartment! His housemate was a 5-ft (1.5-m) long alligator. Owner Antoine Yates said he was trying to create a Garden of Eden.

PAPERED OVER

Old buildings in Virginia are being protected from damage by using toilet paper. Experts say a poultice of toilet paper and water soaks up the salt that destroys bricks. Conservators at Williamsburg historic park used 700 rolls of toilet paper to test the idea on a smokehouse.

Pet Pitch A Japanese real estate agent tried to sell off the last few apartments at a Kawasaki complex in 2002 by offering free puppies and kittens to potential buyers.

Sweating it Out The Panchaiti Shrine in Jalalpur, India, was financed by a loom owner who each day contributed coins equal to the weight of the perspiration from the foreheads of his weavers. In 25 years the hard-working weavers donated 4,000 rupees (about $90 / £50).

Colored lightbulbs are impacted inside 1,000,000 cu ft (30,000 cu m) of ice at the Ice Lantern Festival Exhibition in China. The ice is sculpted into animals and even buildings, such as this mosque.

Cold Comfort

Quebec's newest tourist attraction is a luxurious ice hotel situated on the shores of Lake St. Joseph. Constructed from 4,500 tons of snow and 250 tons of ice, the hotel is rebuilt each year and is open from January until it begins to melt in late March.

The beds are solid blocks of ice with a wooden platform for a foam mattress and there are two art galleries of ice carvings in the form of reliefs projecting from the walls like a frieze. The Grand Hall features a spectacular ice chandelier and in the bar all the furniture and glasses are made of ice. "We don't serve our drinks 'on the rocks'," say the hotel, "we serve them 'in the rocks'!" The N'Ice disco has room for 400 dancers and there is even an ice chapel where "white weddings" take on a whole new meaning!

Rooms at the Ice Hotel, Quebec, average around 27°F (−3°C). Guests keep warm while they sleep by wearing polar fleeces and deer skins.

Sweden also has an ice hotel, which uses 30,000 tons of snow and 10,000 tons of ice.

OFFICE PUT TO SLEEP
An office block in Liverpool, England, was demolished in 2001 because it made people literally sick. The Inland Revenue headquarters at St. John's House was diagnosed as having Sick Building Syndrome after workers complained of a succession of illnesses, including sore throats, runny noses, coughs, and various stress-related symptoms.

Croc Idyllic In the heart of Australia lies a hotel in the shape of a 250-m (820-ft) long crocodile. The Gagudju Crocodile Holiday Inn near Ayers Rock has rooms running along the length of the body to the tail. The swimming pool is situated in the creature's alimentary canal.

Catered Canines In 2000 the Regency Hotel in Manhattan prepared special breakfasts for dogs! The morning feast was served at tables by waiters wearing white gloves and tuxedoes.

Castle of Convenience The Sultan of Brunei's Palace has 1,788 rooms, 257 toilets, and an underground garage for his 153 cars. It would take a visitor over 24 hours, spending 30 seconds in each room, to view the entire palace.

Getting Over It The great bridge of Ceret, France, was built with fines collected from married couples each time they argued. For each quarrel a fine of one centime was collected.

The 1,188-ft (362-m) long "Tibetan Bridge" in Italy is made from just three ropes that connect the island of Procida, near Naples, with Vivara Rock.

Behind Bar Snacks In Beijing, China, there is a restaurant called Chain Cool that has a prison décor. Patrons eat in cells behind iron bars from a menu offering such dishes as "Cruelty" and "Rehabilitation."

Asleep in the Deep
Situated 30 ft (9 m) down in Bora Lagoon in the Florida Keys, Jules' Undersea Lodge is the world's first underwater hotel. A converted underwater research station, it was opened in 1986 and stands on legs 5 ft (1.5 m) off the bottom of the lagoon. To enter, guests, who have included former Canadian Prime Minister Pierre Trudeau and Steve Tyler of the rock band Aerosmith, must scuba dive 21 ft (6.5 m) below the surface of the sea. The hotel boasts a restaurant and two rooms, both with private baths, and can cater for six guests at a time.

Amenities at the Jules' Undersea Lodge, Florida, include a fridge, microwave oven, books, and video recorder, plus a giant porthole to enable guests to observe passing fish.

Index

Index

ACKNOWLEDGMENTS

Jacket (t/l) Sipa/Rex Features; (b/l) Simon Ward/Rex Features; (b/r) Rex Features

8 (t/r) David Hartley/REX, (b) REX; 9 (t) Simon Ward/REX, (b) Yoshikazu Tsuno/AFP/GETTYIMAGE; 10 (t) Sipa Press/REX; 11 (t) Sutcliffe News/REX, (b) Jimin Lai/AFP/GETTYIMAGE; 12 (b) TDY/REX; 13 (t) Anupam Nath/AFP/GETTYIMAGE; 14 (t) Henry McInnes/REX; 15 (t) Toru Yamanaka/AFP/GETTYIMAGE, (b) Ripley's Believe It or Not! Archives, Sony Pictures Television; 16 (t/l) Rabih Mograbi/AFP/GETTYIMAGE, (t/r) AFP/GETTYIMAGE, (b) Jiji Press/AFP/GETTYIMAGE; 17 (t) Nijmegen University/AFP/GETTYIMAGE, (b/l and b/r) Torsten Blackwood/AFP/ GETTYIMAGE; 18 (t) Gero Breloer/AFP/GETTYIMAGE, (b) AFP/GETTYIMAGE; 19 (t) Oregon State University/AFP/GETTYIMAGE; 20 (t and c) Adrian Dennis/ AFP/GETTYIMAGE; 21 (b) Patrick Bernard/AFP/GETTYIMAGE; 22 (t) Nicholas Asfouri/AFP/GETTYIMAGE, (b) Indranil Mukherjee/AFP/GETTYIMAGE; 23 (l) Yoshikazu Tsuno/AFP/GETTYIMAGE; 24 (t) Martial Trezzini/AFP/GETTYIMAGE; 25 (t/l) Mike Nelson/AFP/GETTYIMAGE, (b/r) Yoshikazu Tsuno/ AFP/GETTYIMAGE; 26 (t) AFP/GETTYIMAGE, (b/r) Nigel Snowdon/REX; 27 (t) Gero Breloer/AFP/GETTYIMAGE, (b) AFP/GETTYIMAGE; 28 (t) Hector Mata/APF/GETTYIMAGE, (b/r) Giorgio Benvenuti/AFP/GETTYIMAGE; 29 (t) Courtesy of South West News Service; 30 (t) Jean Pierre Clatot/AFP/GETTYIMAGE; 31 (t) TA/REX; 32 (t) Craig Beruldsen/AFP/GETTYIMAGE, (b/l) Bettmann/Corbis (b/r) Robert Holmes/CORBIS; 33 (b) Frederic J. Brown/AFP/GETTYIMAGE; 34 (t) AFP/GETTYIMAGE, (b) Ludovic Maisant/CORBIS; 35 (t) Ciro Fusco/AFP/GETTYIMAGE, (b) Stephen Frink/CORBIS

All other photos are from Corel, PhotoDisc, Digital Vision and Ripley's Entertainment Inc.